Learning jQuery Toggle Basics

By

Eddie Madrigal, M. Div., M. B. A.

Dedicated to God,
in loving memory of my mom,
Carmen Gutierrez Madrigal
and in gratitude to my darling wife, Erika.
I love you all.

Table of Contents

Chapter 1:

Create a Simple HTML Page

In this chapter, we create our basic HTML page that will be used to help us better understand how jQuery works. Now, because the focus of this tutorial is not on how to compose the most perfect html page, I am simply going to use the following code to help get us started.

With the code looking like this:

```
<!doctype html>

<html>

<head>

<meta charset="utf-8">

<title>jQuery Toggle</title>

</head>

<body>
```

```
</body>

</html>
```

We owe it to ourselves to ask, "What does all of this mean?" Well, let me break the lines down a bit by copying the code above into the section below. With the addition of line numbers that can help better explain what is happening, let's quickly review each of these lines numbers individually.

Line 1: The "<!doctype html>" is required. According to w3.org, "DOCTYPEs are required for legacy reasons. When omitted, browsers tend to use a different rendering mode that is incompatible with some specifications. Including the DOCTYPE in a document ensures that the browser makes a best-effort attempt at following the relevant specifications" (see http://www.w3.org/html/wg/drafts/html/master/syntax.html#the-doctype). In other words, in order to ensure proper a proper and expected viewing experience, always begin your web pages with <!doctype html>.

Line 2: The next element in the html file is the "<html>."

Mozilla.org defines this element as "the HTML Root Element

(<html>) [that] represents the root of an HTML document. All other

elements must be descendants of this element" (see

https://developer.mozilla.org/en-US/docs/Web/HTML/Element/

html). This is especially helpful when we are trying to modify

specific elements on a web page, like when we want to change the

label of a shopping carts button from 'Add to Cart' to 'Remove from

Cart.'

Line 3: Following the <!doctype html> and <html> syntax, we

should tell the browser to load the items found within the "<head>"

section. Because the web page is loaded from top to bottom, it is

important to load particular items on to the client's computer first

before going on to rendering completed web pages. Items like

Cascading Style Sheets that tell browsers how to properly display

colors, font sizes and so forth should be loaded first prior to

displaying the elements they stylize on the page. Also found in this

"<head>" section are metatags that can help search engines better understand your page, which then help them properly rank your site. Lastly, script libraries, like the jQuery JavaScript file that will help your page display properly, can be loaded in here as well.

For our purposes, we will include the source of the jQuery library within the <head> section so that when we use jQuery, we will have the source of the jQuery library ready for use. The <head> section also contains the area where the title of the page can be edited, which can be especially important should you need edit the title of your page.

Line 4: The <meta charset="utf-8"> is used to tell the web browser the specification to use when it comes to handling text information. As Penn State University notes, "if you create a Web site, it is good practice to declare the encoding. Properly encoded Web pages declare the encoding to a browser through a meta tag in the header. Without this tag, a browser may not know to switch to the proper encoding and characters may be displayed as gibberish" (see http://symbolcodes.tlt.psu.edu/web/tips/declare.html)

Line 5: The title tag is used to display the title of the page on web browsers. For our work, we will display the title jQuery Toggle on the top of the web browser like so: <title>jQuery Toggle</title>.

Line 6: When tag elements are no longer required, they should be closed. We indicate an element tag as being closed when we add a forward slash to the tag element, like so: </head>. Basically what we are saying here is, look tag element <head>, we're done with you. And like a period at the end of a sentence, we are going to use the '/' to note the tag elements conclusion. Hence, because we are done with the "<head>" section of our page, we now use </head>.

Line 7: Now comes the body portion of our web page ... the part of the pages that really gets things cooking and onto the client's web browser. The body tag, syntactically written as <body>, is the portion of the page that holds our labels, form elements, submit buttons, paragraphs, titles, borders, and on and on. It is in this

section that we will work our jQuery skills into.

Line 8: Once we are done with the body section of our web page,

we need to close the body tag. Again, using a the forward slash, '/',

we tell the web page that we are now done with the body portion

of the web page … </body>

Line 9: Lastly, when we are done loading the html page onto the

client's web browser, we should close the html file. This is done by

adding the forward slash to the html element, like so </html>.

What we then have, after reviewing lines 1 through 9, is the

following code:

```
<!doctype html>

<html>

<head>

<meta charset="utf-8">

<title>jQuery Toggle</title>
```

```
</head>

<body>

</body>

</html>
```

... which is the code we will work jQuery into as we produce jQuery toggle interactions. But how exactly are we going to add jQuery functionality into a 9-line web page? And, if the jQuery library is so intensely full of lines of code, how are we going easily implement its power into this simple page? The answers coming up in the next chapter.

Notes:

Chapter 2:

Add jQuery Capability

When we get to the point of adding jQuery capability to our web page, it is important to remember that the jQuery library is already built and that all we need to do is learn how to use it (which takes time). Because there are various versions available that can be linked to our site via a 'Content Delivery Network (CDN),' we should take the time to read which version and CDN to use.

For our purposes here, I am going to use the jQuery library link found on jQuery's web site (https://code.jquery.com/) and attach its library to this simple html code by putting it into the head portion of the page.

BEFORE: So, if my pages looks like this:

<!doctype html>

<html>

```
<head>

<meta charset="utf-8">

<title>jQuery Toggle</title>

</head>

<body>

</body>

</html>
```

AFTER: Adding the jQuery library link to the head portion of the page would then look like this:

```
<!doctype html>

<html>

<head>

<meta charset="utf-8">

<title>jQuery Toggle</title>

<script src="https://code.jquery.com/jquery-

1.11.2.min.js"></script>

</head>

<body>
```

```
</body>
</html>
```

Notice that by adding the '<script src="https://code.jquery.com/jquery-1.11.2.min.js"></script>' to the head portion of my website, I am now able to use the jQuery functionality quickly. And, because this booklet is designed to help you better understand the jQuery method, this library must be accessible to the web page.

Now, if you were able to get

```
<!doctype html>
<html>
<head>
<meta charset="utf-8">
<title>jQuery Toggle</title>
<script src="https://code.jquery.com/jquery-
1.11.2.min.js"></script>
</head>
<body>
```

```
</body>

</html>
```

... copied and working on your html page, it only seems logical to test whether or not it really does work. So, what I am going to do now is show how you can quickly send an alert to your users letting them know that, yes, jQuery is in fact working and functioning properly.

For this, I am going to write an alert that displays to the user a message that says: "jQuery Loaded OK!" And should it not load, I will send an alert, saying, "jQuery did not load." To accomplish this, simply write out the following statement into your web pages portion of the <body> tag, like so:

Quick jQuery alert!

```
<script>

$(document).ready(function() {

    if ($) {

        alert("jQuery Loaded OK!");

        } else {
```

```
        alert("jQuery did not load.");

    }

});

</script>
```

What this will then look like when the file is completed should be similar to this:

```
<!doctype html>

<html>

<head>

<meta charset="utf-8">

<title>jQuery Toggle</title>

<script src="https://code.jquery.com/jquery-

1.11.2.min.js"></script>

</head>

<body>

Quick jQuery alert!

<script>

$(document).ready(function() {
```

```
if ($) {

        alert("jQuery Loaded OK!");

    } else {

        alert("jQuery did not load.");

    }

});

</script>

</body>

</html>
```

THE RESULT:

You should see an alert on your web browser similar to the one

shown here ...

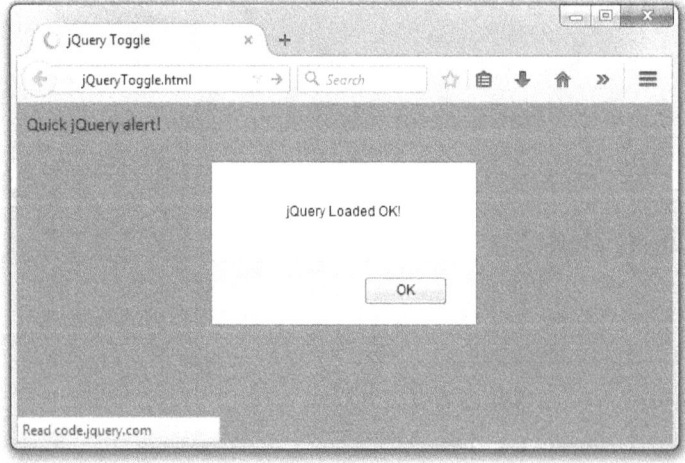

If your code worked out just fine, congratulations! If not, consider checking the code, checking your browser version for compatibility issues as well as your internet connection. Remember, because we are using the jQuery library remotely through a CDN, we need to be connected online. Also note that we do not need to have our site hosted … the page could be written in notepad, saved as 'this is my jQuery file.html' on your desktop, and opened by double clicking it with your mouse.

So, now what? Well, because you have a basic web page working, the jQuery library referenced in the head section of your web page and have checked to make sure it's all working, it's now time to get some elements showing or hiding … starting with a basic understanding of the div, span and id elements that jQuery will show and hide at the click of a mouse. But how, you ask? Go to the next chapter to find out how.

Notes:

Chapter 3:

The div, span and id

When it comes to understanding things that cannot be seen, it can be difficult, if not outright impossible, work with them. This is what often turns people away from really making their pages interactive. Well, my hope will be that by the time you complete this chapter, you will have a clear introduction to div, spans and ids ... as they are crucial basics to modern web pages.

So, what is a div and a span? And how do they relate to an id? Well, if you can imagine a web page that has, for example, a title smack in the middle of your site, like so ...

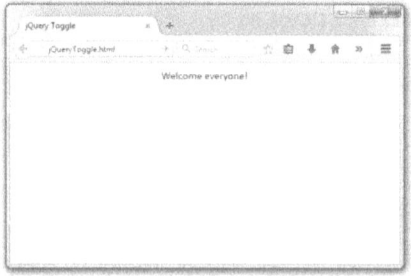

... it could be because of a div container that has been aligned to center and placed in the body portion of your web page. You see, a div is a container, an invisible holder of information that can be given pieces of information within the opening and closing div angle brackets that show information like the one shown above. Div container (short for divider) can even sit in web pages without ever being called to show anything. They are really kind of neat, when you think about them. Additionally, span tag elements can also hold information ... only they display the information in line with the other elements around them.

So, what does the code look like?

```
<!doctype html>
<html>
<head>
<meta charset="utf-8">
<title>jQuery Toggle</title>
<script src="https://code.jquery.com/jquery-
1.11.2.min.js"></script>
```

```
</head>

<body>

<div align="center">

Welcome everyone!

</div>

</body>

</html>
```

Notice that the basics of the web page are the same ... with the only changes being that in the body tag, we put in a div element with an attribute of align and an align value of center. Now, what should also be added (even if you don't think it will be necessary at the time) are id (short of identification, or identifiers). Ids are crucial in your ability to toggle elements on a page because of their uniqueness. In other words, when an id is used on a page, it should only be used once and only once. That way, when your button is click, or a piece of text is hovered over or when the page loads, the id can be found and manipulated quickly and effortlessly. How? Well, let's take a look.

Say you wanted to toggle the phrase from "Welcome everyone!" to "I'm glad you're here!" when a button is clicked on, one of the first things you would want to do is not only create the text, but also create the button that would be used to change the text.

Take a look at the screen shot below.

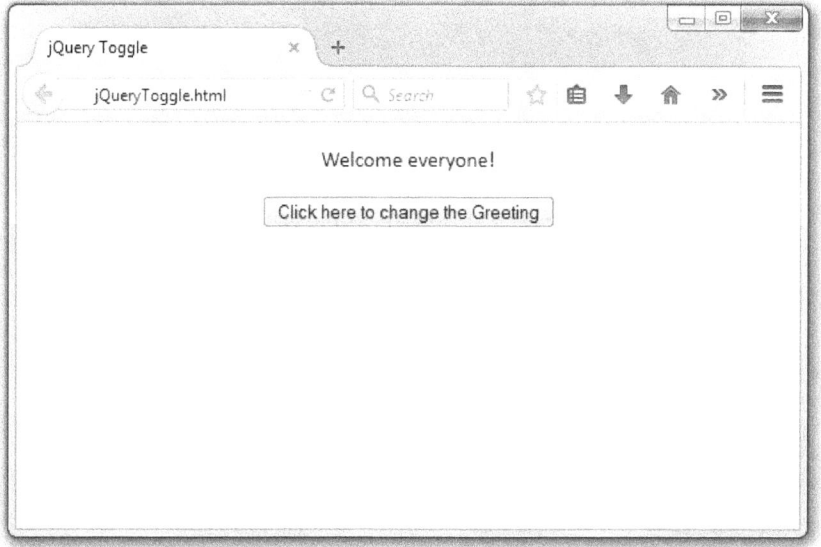

Now, if we were to click on the button labeled, "Click here to change the Greeting," we would get …

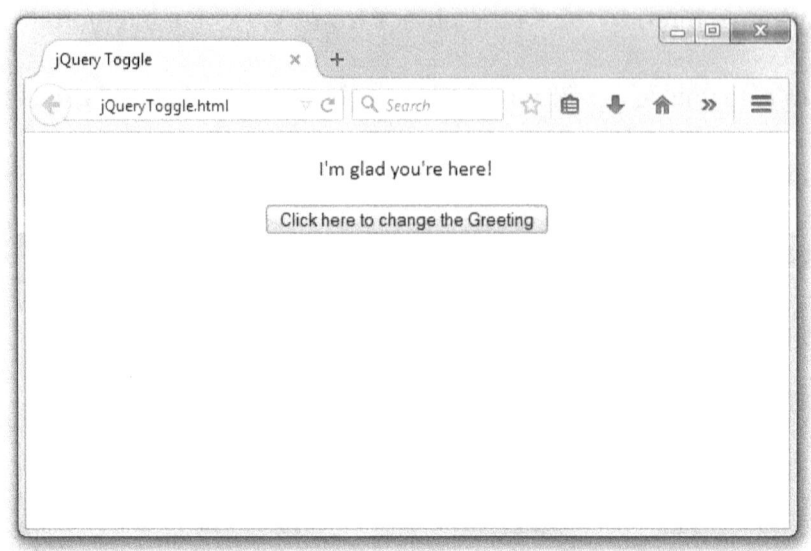

So, now that you can see what happens when the button is clicked,
guess what would happen if you clicked on it again? Yup, you
guessed it … the greeting text would toggle back. Let's take a look
at the code that made this work:

<!doctype html>

<html>

<head>

<meta charset="utf-8">

<title>jQuery Toggle</title>

<script src="https://code.jquery.com/jquery-

1.11.2.min.js"></script>

```html
</head>

<body>

<div align="center">

<p class="mainGreeting">Welcome everyone!</p>

<p class="mainGreeting" style="display: none;">I'm glad you're

here!</p>

</div>

<div align="center">

<button  id="greetingButton">Click here to change the

Greeting</button>

</div>

<script>

$(document).ready(function() {

   $( '#greetingButton' ).click(function() {

        $( '.mainGreeting' ).toggle();

        });

});

</script></body>
```

```html
</html>
```

As you can probably already tell, I created two paragraphs using the <p> tag element and gave them both the same class name, 'mainGreeting.' One of those paragraphs is clearly visible, while the other is not. How? Well, I made them, I told the second one not to display, using the "display: none" inline CSS rule. Then jQuery overrode that command through its toggle() method. I also gave the button an id called "greetingButton" and let jQuery handle the toggling for me when it's clicked.

Again, the thinking is that I need to write two statements that will alternate in display. The first one will be displayed and the second one will not. So then I write:

```html
<p class="mainGreeting">Welcome everyone!</p>
<p class="mainGreeting" style="display: none;">I'm glad you're here!</p>
```

Then, for formatting purposes (in that I want them displayed in the center of the web page), I put them in a centered div using the following line of code: `<div align="center">`

Did I need to give this div an id? No. Could I have added one for later use? Yes. The choice was up to me. How about the use of a span tag element? Couldn't I have used that instead of the div? Of course, no problem. Here's the same code, only instead of using the div tag, I'm using the span.

```
<!doctype html>
<html>
<head>
<meta charset="utf-8">
<title>jQuery Toggle</title>
<script src="https://code.jquery.com/jquery-
1.11.2.min.js"></script>
</head>
<body>
<span style="text-align:center">
<p class="mainGreeting">Welcome everyone!</p>
<p class="mainGreeting" style="display: none;">I'm glad you're
here!</p>
```

```
</span>

<span style="text-align: center; display: block;">

<button  id="greetingButton">Click here to change the

Greeting</button>

</span>

<script>

$(document).ready(function() {

    $( '#greetingButton' ).click(function() {

                $( '.mainGreeting' ).toggle();

        });

});

</script>

</body>

</html>
```

Notice, though, how I had to change the manner in which the span displays content? The div tag comes with a block attribute, in that by default, it will want its own line. A span, however, will simply go with the flow and stay in line with other elements. In other words, div elements stack on top of each other by default while spans, by default, stay in line. For example, here are div elements written side by side but show up stacked one on top of another in a web browser:

Notes:

And here's what I wrote:

```
<!doctype html>

<html>

<head>

<meta charset="utf-8">

<title>jQuery Toggle</title>

<script src="https://code.jquery.com/jquery-

1.11.2.min.js"></script>

<style>

div {

        border: 1px black solid;

        text-align:center;

}

</style>

</head>

<body>

<div>Div 1</div><div>Div 2</div>

<div>Div 3</div>
```

</body>

</html>

In contrast, I wrote the same code … only instead of using the div tag element, I used the span tag element:

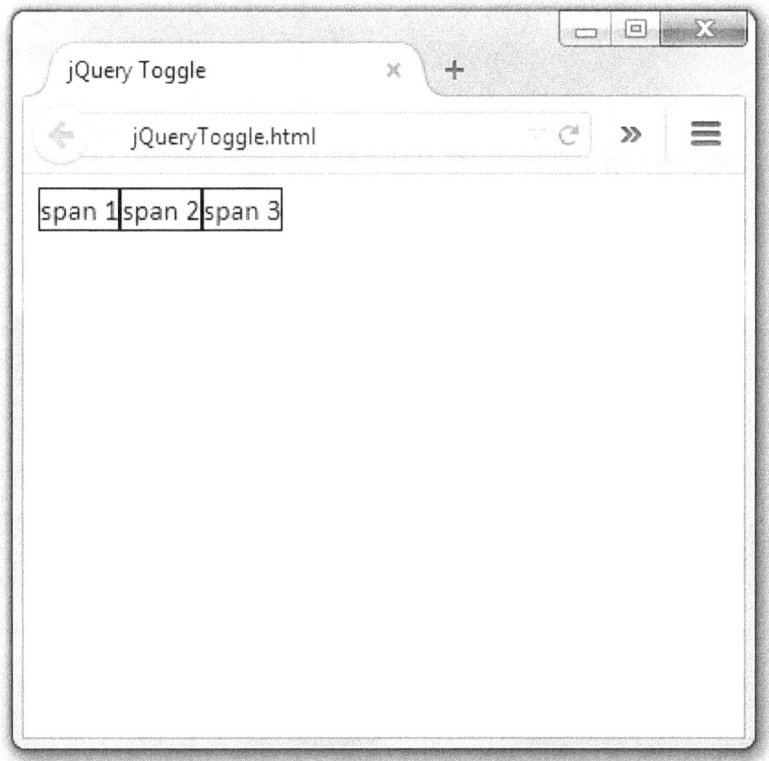

Here the code with the span tag elements instead of the div tag elements:

<!doctype html>

<html>

```html
<head>

<meta charset="utf-8">

<title>jQuery Toggle</title>

<script src="https://code.jquery.com/jquery-

1.11.2.min.js"></script>

<style>

span {

        border: 1px black solid;

        text-align:center;

}

</style>

</head>

<body>

<span>span 1</span><span>span 2</span><span>span 3</span>

</body>

</html>
```

I took the time to write these out so that you can see how each sort of container can be used to display whatever information you want your visitors to leave with.

Now, back to the divs, paragraphs, buttons and clicks. After I wrote the two paragraphs in the centered div, I saved the file and refreshed the web page. When I saw just the first paragraph, I knew I was on the right track. Immediately after checking, I added another div tag and placed a button in it.

```
<div align="center"><button  id="greetingButton">Click here to change the Greeting</button>
</div>
```

This div did not have an id either. Could I have added one? Yes? Again, the choice was mine to make. Now, how do you know when to add one and when to leave one out? The answer comes by knowing if the id will be used later on (as in calculations for a shopping cart, for example). If your answer is no, don't add an id to it. If the answer is maybe or yes, I would add an id to it from the get go.

The last portion I had to deal with was the jQuery code that actually

made this all work. AFTER the page loads the CDN link to the

jQuery library file and AFTER the div and paragraphs are loaded and

AFTER the button is written in the body of the html file BUT before

the ending body tag </body>, I put the jQuery script that makes the

paragraph text change when the button is clicked.

```
<script>
$(document).ready(function() {
    $( '#greetingButton' ).click(function() {
        $( '.mainGreeting' ).toggle();
    });
});
</script>
```

But what about the script itself? What does document dot ready

mean, exactly? What is the dollar sign all about? Well, read the

next chapter to find out.

Notes:

Chapter 4:

Meet the jQuery Script

```
<script>

$(document).ready(function() {

});

</script>
```

When it comes to grasping the idea of the jQuery script, there are a couple of ideas you should both understand and memorize. First is the script tag in the header that links the jQuery library file to your web page.

Memorize: <script

Then: src

Then: =

Then: "

Then, the location of the jQuery file you will be using on your site.

For this book, I used:

https://code.jquery.com/jquery-1.11.2.min.js (which is a link I copied from the http://code.jquery.com web site).

Then I ended the line with double quote, a closing angle bracket and the closing script tag, </script>. This is what I ended up putting in the head portion of my web page.

```
<script src="https://code.jquery.com/jquery-1.11.2.min.js"></script>
```

The second item I would encourage you to follow is to put the script that will be doing jQuery work towards the bottom of the web page, just before the closing body tag, </body>. This way, because your page loads from top to bottom, you will know for sure that your html tag elements will be loaded prior to your script looking to use them. This is the main reason why I use the following right before and after my script tags:

```
<script>
$(document).ready(function() {
```

```
    $( '#greetingButton' ).click(function() {

        $( '.mainGreeting' ).toggle();

    });

});

</script>
```

Well, what does all of this mean? It means that when the page

loads, again from top to bottom, the browser (Microsoft Internet

Explorer, Mozilla Firefox, Google Chrome, Apple Safari, etc.) will in

turn encounter the script tag, <script>. The browser then knows

that there is a script coming up and that chances are high that the

script coming up will be JavaScript (which is what we want, seeing

that jQuery is a JavaScript library. The, browser will encounter the

page's first jQuery line of code, $.

Now, the $ sign is the same as writing out the word, jQuery. Only,

instead of using jQuery, I used $. Same difference, and certainly

nothing mysterious. To prove this point, I rewrote the toggle code

we've been working with the jQuery word instead.

```html
<!doctype html>

<html>

<head>

<meta charset="utf-8">

<title>jQuery Toggle</title>

<script src="https://code.jquery.com/jquery-

1.11.2.min.js"></script>

</head>

<body>

<span style="text-align:center">

<p class="mainGreeting">Welcome everyone!</p>

<p class="mainGreeting" style="display: none;">I'm glad you're

here!</p>

</span>

<span style="text-align: center; display: block;">

<button id="greetingButton">Click here to change the

Greeting</button>

</span>
```

```
<script>

jQuery(document).ready(function() {

    jQuery( '#greetingButton' ).click(function() {

        jQuery( '.mainGreeting' ).toggle();

        });

});

</script>

</body>

</html>
```

The next portion of code, this time from left to right, is the word document. What this means is that the script will not run until the html file, or document, is ready to be worked on. In other words, don't run the script until the file has completely loaded onto the client's machine. Then, when the document is loaded and is ready to be used, the client's browser is instructed to then run a function, noted by the word, function. (Simple, right??).

Now comes the nifty stuff. Once the document is ready, it will just

sit there until an event of some kind happens. An event? An event

like a wedding, a concert, a birthday part? Well, sort of. Let me

first define what an event is. An event is something that happens

that would not ordinarily happen. In this particular example, a click

would be considered an event. Why? Because had the html

document loaded on its own and without your clicking on the

button, nothing extraordinary would have happened. In this, then,

clicking on the button is an event, that in turn causes (or triggers)

something else to happen … in this case, the toggle.

But how does the computer know what to toggle and how? Well,

again, looking at the code, from top to bottom and from left to

right, you will notice the following syntax:

$('# …

What this is say is, jQuery, go and select the contents within the

parenthesis, starting with what is in the quotes and look for the id …

But why the #? This is so that jQuery looks for an id. Yes, the '#' is

the symbol used for id.

Going forward, we notice that jQuery now looks for the id called

"greetingButton," which is what used to identify the button

specifically that when clicked will cause the toggle on the class

"mainGreeting" to run.

```
jQuery( '#greetingButton' ).click(function() {

        jQuery( '.mainGreeting' ).toggle();

});
```

If it helps, try running the code. If it works, great. Now, memorize.

This sort of jQuery toggle coding is very, very common.

When the browser gets to the line that ends with the toggle();, you

know that whatever is in the .mainGreeting class will either display

or hide, depending on the state that it is in when the button was

first clicked.

Notes:

Chapter 5:

Show and Hide with Toggle

Now that we have some jQuery, Toggle, div, span, id, CSS, and so on items out of the way, let's take a look at how we can make items like:

- Showing or hiding more information, slowly, when a 'More Info' link is pressed?

- Showing or hiding information about a product or service, depending on the image pressed.

- Changing the text of a button when it is pressed.

Let's take a look at the first one. When we talk about showing or hiding tables, we are basically talking about whether an element, in this case, a table will have a display attribute of none or not. Tables, of course, will also need an id and the web page will need some sort of event to listen for (click, mouseover, etc.) in order to trigger jQuery.

For this example, I have modified the code we've been working with, only this time, tables with a border of 1px will be shown or hidden, depending on the toggle:

```
<!doctype html>

<html>

<head>

<meta charset="utf-8">

<title>jQuery Toggle</title>

<script src="https://code.jquery.com/jquery-
1.11.2.min.js"></script>

</head>

<body>
```

```html
<div>

<table align="center" style="border: 1px black solid;"

class="mainGreeting"><tr><td>Welcome

everyone!</td></tr></table>

<table align="center" style="border: 1px black solid; display: none;"

class="mainGreeting"><tr><td>I'm glad you're

here!</td></tr></table>

</div>

<div style="text-align: center">

<button  id="greetingButton">Click here to change the

Greeting</button>

</div>

<script>

jQuery(document).ready(function() {

   jQuery( '#greetingButton' ).click(function() {

       jQuery( '.mainGreeting' ).toggle();

       });

});
```

```
</script>

</body>

</html>
```
Notice that aside from some CSS and changing the paragraph tag elements <p> into tables, with a row and a column <table><tr><td>, it's basically the programming logic … with nothing in the <script> tags changing.

How about showing or hiding more information, slowly, when a 'More Info' link is pressed? How would that work? How about showing a 'Less Info' link show when you want to close the additional text? Well, here you go. Let's see if you can follow what is happening here …

```
<!doctype html>

<html>

<head>

<meta charset="utf-8">

<title>jQuery Toggle</title>

<script src="https://code.jquery.com/jquery-
1.11.2.min.js"></script>
```

```html
</head>

<body>

<div align="center">

<br />To be, or not to be: that is the question:

<br />Whether 'tis nobler in the mind to suffer

<br />The slings and arrows of outrageous fortune,

<br />Or to take arms against a sea of troubles,

<br />And by opposing end them? To die: to sleep;

<br />No more; and by a sleep to say we end

<br />The heart-ache and the thousand natural shocks

<br />That flesh is heir to, 'tis a consummation

<br />Devoutly to be wish'd. To die, to sleep;

<br />To sleep: perchance to dream: ay, there's the rub;

<div class="infoP2">[More Info ...]</div>

<div class="infoP2" style="display:none;">[Less Info ...]</div>

</div>

<div align="center" id="secondP" style="display:none;">

<br />For in that sleep of death what dreams may come
```


When we have shuffled off this mortal coil,

Must give us pause: there's the respect

That makes calamity of so long life;

For who would bear the whips and scorns of time,

The oppressor's wrong, the proud man's contumely,

The pangs of despised love, the law's delay,

The insolence of office and the spurns

That patient merit of the unworthy takes,

When he himself might his quietus make

<div class="infoP3">[More Info ...]</div>

<div class="infoP3" style="display:none;">[Less Info ...]</div>

</div>

<div align="center" id="thirdP" style="display: none">

With a bare bodkin? who would fardels bear,

To grunt and sweat under a weary life,

But that the dread of something after death,

The undiscover'd country from whose bourn

No traveller returns, puzzles the will

And makes us rather bear those ills we have

Than fly to others that we know not of?

Thus conscience does make cowards of us all;

And thus the native hue of resolution

Is sicklied o'er with the pale cast of thought,

And enterprises of great pith and moment

With this regard their currents turn awry,

And lose the name of action. - Soft you now!

The fair Ophelia! Nymph, in thy orisons

Be all my sins remember'd.

</div>

</div>

<script>

```
$(document).ready(function() {

  $( '.infoP2' ).click(function() {

            $( '#secondP' ).toggle( 'slow' );

            $( '.infoP2').toggle( 'slow' );

      });
```

```
       $( '.infoP3' ).click(function() {

              $( '#thirdP' ).toggle( 'slow' );

              $( '.infoP3').toggle( 'slow' );

       });

});

</script>

</body>

</html>
```

Following the logic we have been using so far, the jQuery seems to

be showing and hiding text via the Toggle method, and then

changing from [More Info] to [Less Info].

How about changing the content on a page depending on whether

one image instead of another was clicked on. How would that look

like? Are there similarities in the code being used? Let's see.

Guess what is going on here?

```
<!doctype html>

<html>

<head>
```

```html
<meta charset="utf-8">

<title>jQuery Toggle</title>

<script src="https://code.jquery.com/jquery-

1.11.2.min.js"></script>

<style>

img {

        width: 50px;

}

</style>

</head>

<body>

<div align="center">

<p class="shoppingCart">Add to Cart <br /><img

src="plus.png"><br>Purchase now and save 10%!</p>

<p class="shoppingCart" style="display:none;">Remove from Cart

<br /><img src="minus.png"><br />All prices are guaranteed or your

money back!</p>

</div>
```

```
<script>

        $(document).ready(function() {

    $('.shoppingCart').click( function() {

                        $('.shoppingCart').toggle ( 'slow' );

            });

    });

</script>

</body>

</html>
```

When the image in the Add to Cart portion of the page is clicked,

the image is swapped out

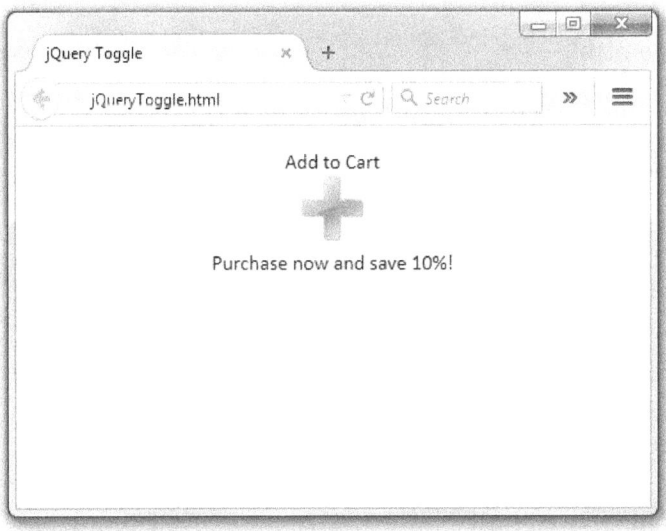

with one that has a minus; the text is changed to Remove from Cart

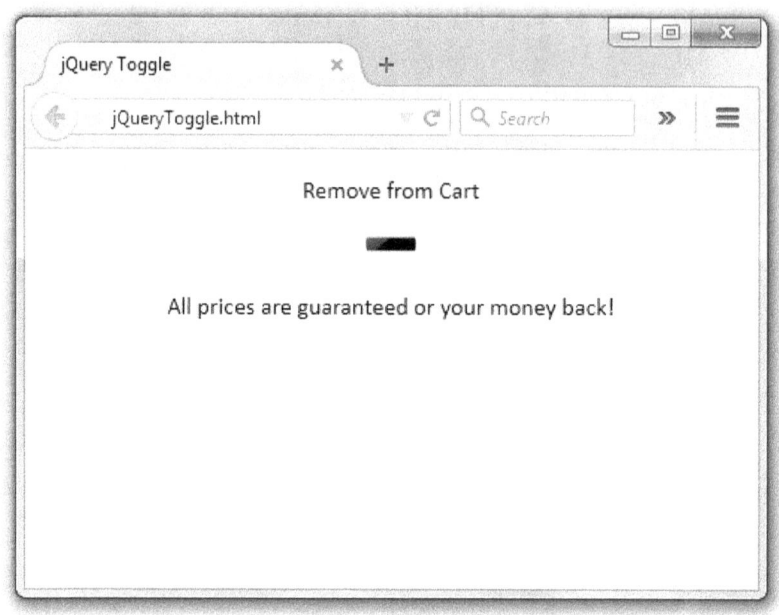

Finally, you can change the text of a button when, say, someone is buying an item from your online store.

<!doctype html>

<html>

<head>

<meta charset="utf-8">

<title>jQuery Toggle</title>

<script src="https://code.jquery.com/jquery-

1.11.2.min.js"></script>

```
<style>
img {

        width: 50px;

}
</style>
</head>
<body>
<div align="center">Something for sale
<button class="btnCart">Add to Cart</button>
<button class="btnCart" style="display:none;">Remove from
Cart</button>
</div>
<script>
        $(document).ready(function() {
    $('.btnCart').click( function() {
                        $('.btnCart').toggle ();
                });
    });
```

```
</script>

</body>

</html>
```

Notice that the same concept of toggling items that are initially display to then being displayed is what we are using the jQuery toggle method for?

Keep practicing … and you'll soon be writing up your own jQuery in no time.

Chapter 6:

Conclusion

As you can see, using jQuery's toggle capability can help you greatly increase the interactivity your site can have with those visiting the page. Not only will you be able to show and hide html tag elements, but you will be able to provide a great means by which your visitors experience your site.

If you have any questions, please feel free to email me at edmadrigal@yahoo.com. You can also look me up on Facebook at http://facebook.com/familiaMadrigal.

References

Art of Europe. (2015). *Art of Europe*.

http://www.artofeurope.com/shakespeare/sha8.htm

Mozilla Developer Network (MDN). *<html>*.

https://developer.mozilla.org/en-

US/docs/Web/HTML/Element/html

Penn State. (2015). *Declare the Encoding*.

http://symbolcodes.tlt.psu.edu/web/tips/declare.html

W3C. (2015). *HTML 5.1 Nightly*.

http://www.w3.org/html/wg/drafts/html/master/syntax.ht

ml#the-doctype

www.ingramcontent.com/pod-product-compliance
Lightning Source LLC
Chambersburg PA
CBHW071003180526
45168CB00003B/1263